PLAN B

PLAN B

by

Augustus Carleton

to my friend and fellow
author, [illegible]
[illegible] & good
[illegible] & camaraderie
[illegible]
[illegible]
04/09/13

THREE RAIL PRESS, SEATTLE

for Maggie

PLAN B

Contents

Beautiful Planet	9
Becalming the Waters	10
Blue Angel	11
Comfort Letter	12
Defined Terms	13
Ebey's Landing	14
Enough About You	15
Feel the Benefits	16
Formula One	17
Garden Varieties	18
Getting There As Half the Fun From Here	19
Getting to Know You	20
Global Proportions	21
Good Seats	22
Happy to Be Here	23
I've Learned From All of This	24
Job One	25
A Kind of Federal Paradise	26
Late in the Century	27
Leading Indicators	28
Long Hours	29
Misdirection	30
More Than Available	31
The Next Step	32

No Real Peace	33
The Oak Room	34
Oh, Lucky Day	35
The Old Masters	36
Once Around the Lake	37
Plan B	38
The Playdate	39
Problems of Scale	40
The Quarter Ended	41
Remembrance	42
Restrictive Legend	43
Rogue Wave	44
Secrets of Filmmaking	45
Select Imprint	46
The Ship of Right Suggestion	47
Social Grace	48
South San Francisco	49
Standard Time	50
Surface Mining	51
Tender Offer	52
A Troubled Country Heard From	53
Up Against It	54
Very Nearly Yours	55
What You're Willing to Do	56

PLAN B

Beautiful Planet

You might have the same crisis reaction
To *bad* news, so relax, establishment
Is out of your mind and at the printer's.
After weeks of longing, the day cloudless,
The neighborhood waiting to serve breakfast,
The street scene markedly unsuburban,
Now events conspire to resist resist-
Ance to rest. Flip through the options: inquire
Of deep, principled thinkers what they would
Recommend for someone of completely
Disparate principles; untangle lawnchairs
And sag; appreciate offerings of chefs;
Watch and remark of your watchful children
How they embody the life you most love.

Becalming the Waters

And when reticence was found out sideways,
Bright, knowing menus of success dropped down,
Smack in the parking lot of industry,
Like a paratrooper to a schoolyard
At recess, with one girl who would marvel
The tableaux for the rest of her childhood.
Choices re-presented represented
A new way, with old feeling, and the same
Trepidation (though managed) that the job
Flashed at the interview when unsecured;
So the gift that was thought lost reappeared
In fresh wrapping, like the current fashion
That won't date its snapshot appearance, yet,
And how you once knew to sing found a song.

Blue Angel

Turns out they were in league with cheerleaders,
A fact that's been checked on by culturally
Hardnosed internationalists who lugged
Groceries by cart when living in Dublin.
Room's tight too in the natural atmosphere,
Too dear to suppose a place set for all,
Or for each, or for me, for that matter
Bar-coded for swiping like law firm files.

I loved our formation, until the lure
Of yon hillside light tore my wingtip from
Yours and I barreled into my own thing,
Leaving mom and dad behind the border
On a farm that recedes in my smoketrail.
It accelerates, just the cheek of it.

Comfort Letter

Now everyone's coping wonderfully,
Spanning gamuts, spinning wheels, frosting cakes.
One guy was unabashed, and that by turns
Seemed embarrassing, forthright, downright rude;
But don't hope for the lesson to be drawn
To your portfolio. It's discovered
That the travel between the chosen and
Picked-on poles is a stress to be countered
Through diet, exercise and strict routine,
Propped like mattresses against the deluge.
There's a mail slot where at odd times of day
Messages like this pushed at twice sound speed
Will decompress, debrief and quarantine
Themselves back to health before they're opened.

Defined Terms

We thought to run a controversial ad,
Capitalize on the lack of remorse
That seems to be getting people funded
Lately. Sure, recruits shrink, shriek from highwire
Trajectories to which the fine print binds them,
Antics some won't shirk, by the way. New ways
Slip in under low horizons you can't
Scan anymore for the proper posture
Your own matriculation in the g-
Force training pressed you to as legacy.
But let us not speak for the manual,
Which comes in handy and is three hole punched
For ease of discard should revolution
Unseat particular sections, as tabbed.

Ebey's Landing

As to whether a flower is native
Earth is indifferent, I think, if you know
Earth as knowing; even a "weed" that spreads
Like a colony, unlike colonists,
Contributes a nature earth can live with.
The death of the last elm moves not mountains,
It only breaks hearts. The care of the heart,
However, is the earth's spirit's tender.

The settler finds prairie but sees farmland,
Not discerning (I imagine) what woods
Or salmon runs a people past (or else
Destined to return through a channel maze)
Gave chase to. But to what different vale of
Present seem the tidepool and the killdeer.

Enough About You

Honing in on love, not a risk in sight,
The sabotage appears to have taken.
Tomorrow's a new rule, stakeouts will be
Reorganized again, supposedly

To stay competitive, whether I heed
Advice slung from sultry melodies
Or not. You know what I mean. Microphones
Amplify these sorts of whispers. No good

Comes of it usually though no one's wise,
The keys are in the public library
Off-line and might be grabbed while no one pays
A farthing of attention; and none do.

Tonight we'll brook transition together.
For now, the tools intend their chosen trades.

Feel the Benefits

A well planned operation, like a sun
Salutation, or a shrewd entrapment,
Or a public company meeting its
Analysts' expectations, represents
An economy folks can map their days
Around between hirings and upheavals,
Solar storms, affirmative defenses,
Misgivings that align into upsets.

Though we were suited to the arrangement,
Threads of subtext later shrank in the wash.
Flowers blossomed and anniversaries
Piled on, we thought, but when you actually
Counted one hand was oddly sufficient.
The deepest beliefs were wrapped in syntax.

Formula One

It doesn't have to be sad forever.
You'll sin again, and there'll be forgiveness
As long as you don't take it for granted.
And the wry tone that wends you new places
Bears an aspect of shining city you'll
Never leave, nor need to, as it happens.
Even now the drifting weight of the world,
That takes a seat inside your two, snug doors,
Groans like a bamboozlement, a hoodwink,
Strangely presaging a tour of delight,
Like learning that Formula One savvy
Euro-road master Andrettis repair
Year after year to a family stock
Car compound in Nazareth, Pennsylvania.

Garden Varieties

One of the accidental mysteries
Of the buildout is our hall's curvature,
Lending a feel of tossed trajectory
To all comers from an end that merely
  Echoes.

    Great shakes!

      Messengers have always
Rocked at will the train of my swivel chair
Thoughts, no less fantastic than Manhattans
Of flexible business bedfellows, tuned,
Like me, to faults or arguable virtues.
But when the mental life commands more than
Sassy zeros at the end of a string,
I'll lay in in a workmanlike manner,
Like floor tile, a discipline of rhythms,
Like a school with spring and fall semesters.

Getting There As Half the Fun From Here

Summer ended when the last brush of stain
Seeped into the deck even as the first
Autumn rain fell. Usually a border
Gets crossed before you know where you're going,
Lights, sirens, if there are to be any,
Wash back to a constructive notice we
Sheepishly admit we're conversant with.
This entails jail time or group therapy
Or stolen vacations where she'd behave
Better for he who is minding the fort,
Except he forgives. He's mowing the lawn,
Taking the kids to school, breaking the bread.
What the hand finds to do, the heart follows,
Reluctant or willing, now or for good.

Getting to Know You

And then quite simply you were accustomed
To automatic transmission, meter
Parking with the right change in your pocket,
Girls or boys meeting your look with a smile.
Global political implications
Resounded which you would tease out somehow,
And soon, in the comfort of your own skin
The better to travel as your mind strayed
Open (hopefully) and expressive of
Values you might lend a name to later.
Down the road, still oddly patchwork-mended
And rural in spite of overarching
Patterns of distribution, differences
Have compromised to fit you well enough.

Global Proportions

The moon at the end of the avenue
Outruns the miles in our minivan, takes
A national spaceship to travel to,
Practically, yet orbits predictably,

We think, expressing an attraction far
Too vast and constant to be elegant,
Showing up at cross streets, throwing brand name
Drive-throughs in a natural light that makes them

More impermanent, less than organic,
Appointed briefly for an errand, like
Military commissaries, slapped up,
As temporary as weeded gardens.

O moon, how also fragile human love,
That earthly gravitation we regard!

Good Seats

Almost at once, you knew the exception
Would rule the terms of the conversation,
Absolve public agencies from wiping
Things down or feathering to the bare wood.
They weren't as interested in memories
Per se as in what such blocked on the stage
Of perception, programmed the dimension,
Even, in which the choreography
Would be seen, heard, the dust of it tasted
Rising from the floorboards straining their nails.
Time couldn't be scheduled on any grid,
So it meant faith to leave a deposit
On the hall and talk directions later.
There's a lot of fun in what you're wearing.

Happy to Be Here

No sooner do you tour the English house
Than some Darcy purporting to be lord
Turns up to point out portrait likenesses
And moves in to implore you to be mistress.
The problem is, you feel the business plan
Behind the hospitality. Details
Are glued with glitter on the edges, like
Mints on the pillows, lemons in the beer,
Baubles you might aestheticize, except
The management won't take it lying down.
So life displays the contours of a word.
The left and right of another's success
Realign, some, at the drop of a hat,
The twist of a screw, the shock of what is true.

I've Learned From All of This

The consequences were like a party,
Something to be endured, to mingle through
Even as the overstretched young people
Let loose their resentments, to the delight
Of middle aged men who fancy themselves
In charge, suave, like some shade of Kennedy.
Then we girls went home, each unto her own
Fiefdom or unincorporated scrape,
Planning to return the dress worn but once,
Showing for jobs the next day, the hallway
Hellos with the first pass, and tight lipped smiles
On the next out of custom, or terror
That one's religion, fount of all one's love,
Would indict the act of unthinking work.

Job One

Thinking better of their invitations,
People left work hours ago. I stepped in
When the architect died and the heathen
Fashioned glass with groovy tints for Lever
House. Soon all corners of the box will close
And combs and shaving brushes swell in size
As clouds and blue sky wrap around the walls
Whence floorboards vanish like telegraph wires.

Will any of this play in the sculpture
Garden late summer recital Friday
Nights among the Calders and the roped-off
Lipschitz? The crowd's fickle, and the snotty
Put down at the exit gate that squeezes
Light in the glossy column inches counts.

A Kind of Federal Paradise

Life's cool in the gated community.
A quaint overabundance of signage,
Like bric-a-brac in a bed & breakfast,
Extols behaviors in proper spaces.
One sleeps well, just knowing emergency
Eye wash stations sport international
Safety icons recognized instantly
All the straight length of a freshly waxed hall.

Performing garden critical functions
With walkie talkies and water hoses,
Only the groundscrew, guardsmen of edges
Of sidewalks from the green, creeping ivy,
Labor the installation on Sunday,
Their trucks parked in slips unreserved weekends.

Late in the Century

Records became too easy to record.
Clerks would file anything you handed them.
You could post your own web page off the shelf.
Type could be cast and broken virtually
Electronically, it held heft no more
No more. The system was left unguarded.
Secretaries of state would register
D/b/a's without checking prior rights.

As you'd imagine, many lamented,
Many lauded, the passing of pleading
Strictures and white space requirements. It
Mattered again what you happened to say,
Naught to shrift on, except maybe the style
Sheets survived translated from memory.

Leading Indicators

As we crawl back into the box, we hold
The thought outside for subsequent field trips
Or restraining orders we might author,
If the truth be known and the prospects fair.
European concepts like bicycled
Police or butter pressed in tiny crocks
Find import, to no lack of bemusement
On our brand strategic shores, for sure, but
Sales flatten even as consumers sour
On uninflected, spiritual ideas.
Mirrors, now more reflective than normal,
Slow gestures down to a virtual crawl,
And in conference rooms the conversation
Plays itself out out of force of routine.

Long Hours

Office work is one relentless season
Marked by no arrival, tinged with no loss,
Lauding or conceding no migration,
Relegating calendars to paper
Kept in case of threatened audits, lawsuits.
No one is expected at the manor
Holidays; there are no holidays, but
Mere vacations squeezed in tight to no rhyme
Or to crass "observed" Mondays stringing
Third days to the weekend now and then, more
Time to squander, to be made up later.
Office years do not repeat. Remember
Years the summer lingered, winter tarried?
Even wars had fall and spring campaigns, once.

Misdirection

He has to speak to get the meter right,
Though better lines are those he doesn't force.
And like a string that runs a lifted kite
He speeds along a self rewarding course.
What difference he might make to save her hopes
Is not a matter taken by his care.
She has her job. The family simply copes
And in their lives may well be unaware
Of all the lofty purpose he sustains.
Although he speaks, he whispers to himself
And to the bookish, paper thin remains
That lay in sheaves on table top or shelf.
It's not for me to judge him on the rest.
One ought to heed the voice one welcomes best.

More Than Available

A summer attitude fell upon us
And we eyed each other questioningly.
It was possible to rest trust on facts
Or a pattern of past behavior and
Not cede weight to the language the body
Communicated in passing, for sure.
Perhaps we would visit later and pick
Up side-stepping the wordless encounter
Between. The air's warm. In elevators
People confide the trouble they're having
Sleeping nights, even with windows open.
We will move this discussion out of doors.
The story of today will shift tenses,
The season arrive like new history.

The Next Step

Finally, it wasn't necessary
To train all energy to a focus,
But happiness instead arrived like rain,
Fragrant and electric and refracted,
And when the pending tasks the motherboard
Forbore as "wholly outside your control"
Came to feel like the hard knocks, taking and
Especially giving at the margins,
You figured all along they could become,
There was a leisure that might prepare you
Or a palette for a museum blue
Period viewers would gasp at later.
That's how custom survived bad precedents
And suspense replaced pure, cruel surprise.

No Real Peace

It's here, look around you! No, not that page!
Little turns quite like the optimal world.
A prayer of mental gratitude equips
You to guess why deference is specified:

Seating arrangements trying discussion,
Quotes rounding out the truth of a fact sheet,
Tax tail wagging the business deal doggie,
Contents shifting on planes, buses, subways –

All common, daily instances of stuff
We implement and fade away from, still
Dripping suspicious, on to the next thing.
Life lops off stuck up golden digits, we

Know, conveyor belts leavings to distant
Recycling programs no one understands.

The Oak Room

The city is a place where people touch
Where streets are grimy and clothing formal
Where mixed drinks are usually in fashion
Where waiters negotiate paneled rooms

Rooms that sigh with the absence of artists
Who died here penniless, pneumatic, long
Before their work composed our mental life
Where nice girls from British Columbia

Sing in clubs from albums out next Tuesday
Where iambs have the proper stage to walk
Where strangers call you by your proper name
And repartee permits some vulgar verbs

That you may come and go without restriction
The city's intimate, indifferent, real

Oh, Lucky Day

Though you were tentative as usual,
Outcomes stepped from their decisiveness steep,
Dried off, and felt like living. No caffeine
Juice or headache for the lack of any,
Enough baby fat to pillow hunger,
Phone calls galore, and none directed me.
But this is about you, your ambition
And the friendship between us we might stare
Dumbfounded at in new newsprint when you
Or I get forwarded for President
And attributions multiply like lies.
Today, nothing's crucial or certain, just
Slow, the way paint dries, quick, how dry paint moves,
All at once, like a tightly stretched canvas.

The Old Masters

Their language was so convincing, we swooned:
They must have lived in some sort of era,
Walked around when streets were still swept with brooms
And read verse to each other over beer.

Now their valets are talking. What a shame
Ready money floated only lately
And then to sponsor lurid, hall of fame
Sagas told improbably politely;

It underserves the human composure
We select recognize in them, latent
Like canistered film waiting exposure.
Their poems are like well-drafted patents.

And now the halls fall silent, in homage
To lines that crossed their minds but missed the page.

Once Around the Lake

Here's my commitment: every other day
I'll run by you counterclockwise. Decide
Soon, please, if you would, whether an inhouse
Or outsourced outreach effort's quickest.
No question we'll employ all resources
Because this is what the high road requires.

Covering terrain, improvising tools,
Taking a wallop of humility
To the head to flush out arrogance, wow,
This is the big, expanded agenda
Mother told us about when I was *the*
Favored child, but you're the successful one,
Today. Look what I scatter for keeping
My own green counsel, the fruit yet to come.

Plan B

All thirty odd days of the month expired
And the deal remained on the table, made
Due with its surroundings, set up camp, pitched
A tarp to cover the canteen, practiced
Variations of old, opening moves:
Pawn to king four, knight to queen's bishop three.
Someone folded, laid out, colored, paper
To be a stream to fish in, wade across.
And so by slow gradients and degrees
The dreams of the city rolled away, tight
Disclosure seemed ever more practical,
Ever less necessary. Periods
Went waiting or dividing somewhere else,
The currency begging new exchanges.

The Playdate

Since first arranging the playdate, daily
Things like laundry and shuttles to the air-
Port crowded my attention from the star
I'd so consciously calendared in red.
And then that morning I couldn't even
Navigate the stairs before the last ring
Kicked your reminding call into voice mail,
Twice! Ah well, what mattered is that we worked
The kids together around our excess
Distractions and explanations, awkward
Inasmuch as they make us seem lonely
To each other at the point of hand-off.
Off you whisked in your Volvo with my five-
Year old and your own snugly buckled in.

Problems of Scale

The land will wear the etymologies
Bestowed by locals and federal workers
Stuck out there, switching thin, essential lines
That light long distant, unshuttered cities.

Getting from there to here, or where to where,
After terrain absolves itself of trees,
Small flat forevers, between unmeeting
Arcs of irrigation, beg transition.

We passed through a town (reduced speed ahead)
And spied a child with hair so red, I thought
We'll find her here again by asking, if
We come again and stop awhile to ask.

Distinguishing two inclines of climate,
We drive home the one, true, vanishing point.

The Quarter Ended

Heroes are those who handle but don't mark
The sadness borne by most accoutrements
As well as stuff folks foot and fetishize
And grow old with, like stale receivables.

More proper empathy is fair regard,
Like knowing how to sucker punch a client
Or double speak the way good partners do,
Flouting public signals for private gain,

Or like reducing intangible trade
Secrets to practice, but not their products,
Chickens in pots, computers in houses,
Those spoils as gifts that keep on marketing.

One shoe's no sooner on than the other
Drops, like gross profit beneath gross margin.

Remembrance

Then I thought of you, whether you could mean
To me how you once did, and by the time
The infrastructure for the railroad or
Interstate highway system or wired or
Satellite transmission made far distance
The table for reaching an arm across
That clever folk sooner know to figure,
Your name rode the waves or particles or
Box cars, bought a purchase on an address
That made my heart race just to recognize.
Believe you, it was only confusion
That consigned me to an opposite coast
All these years. Our shores seem easy enough
To collapse, now that we're touching again.

Restrictive Legend

Put out to catch yourself in your own net,
You wind your boat and your back from the shore,
Leaving harbingers to work the phone tree,
Risking homecoming to a deal crater
On the very lot with beachfront permits.
"They," wallowed in all that surplus background,
Turn tasks turnable in bankers' hours.
Might that speak discipline off which to bounce?

Should you un-dog ear all squirreled away leads?
Navigate maps in real time? Land to land
With its old ranges? New concave contours?
And second minute by minute motions
Of an indigenous weather pattern
That floods to local effects each comer?

Rogue Wave

Weeds popped in the cracks of expectations
As the better adjusted precedents
Put on the laurels of proper manners.
This took years to shape, literally, or
One cookie spin on the spit that's a beach.
We tried naming disappointment "relief"
But reputation had conceded us,
Forcing our guts and minds into escrow,
There to float, like arms of an astronaut.
Who'd rely on distraction for focus?
Aside from myopic entrepreneurs
Who countenance change in a reductive
Fear of what the good life must be hiding?
You have but one slim weekend to connect.

Secrets of Filmmaking

Introspection is its own element,
The close framing of time its own reward.
Living is never captured. Images
Are as transient as the permanent
Twilight of a northern spring evening,
A means to find a feeling way to think,
A profession of faith, a devotion
Attracting disciples and keeping some.

Look, the children here appreciate things,
They pair small stones by contrasting colors,
Curate shells on a favored driftwood plank,
Build blocks between rungs of the central stairs.
Whatever a camera might do, they track
The grain that feeds the hunger in the eye.

Select Imprint

Days of extraordinary effort
But the river finds the smallest misplaced
Word to wear against and leak around. An
Accident of the appointive process
Which is par for the ordinary course
Of commercial life, the way we transact
Now and the mirror we brandish, parade
Ritualistically. Evaluate
My own motives and I find I almost
Have to borrow someone else's to do
As the river and toss up wisecracks like
I'm born to it. This is not sloppy so
Much as a winning accommodation
To the pace that's set, the loves we placate.

The Ship of Right Suggestion

How sweetly learned, horny courtiers
Did pencil circumstance of rowdy lives!
Succession telescoped dramatically
Might best be illustrated in my age
By the rapid replacement of film stocks
For the big screen, each cheapening the last
In certain patrons' eyes, dating movies
By fine gradations of decades, wholly
Apart from then prevailing "production
Values" and other nonsense expenses.
But I stray from the moral betterment
Of the subject at large, the destiny
That questions destiny in all modern
Climates of past, present and each to come.

Social Grace

I've walked this way before, and then I've paused.
And now I lope or amble as social
Mores dictate or the mood strikes, no more
Follows one cause than the other when I
Just leave out how driven everyone is,
Don't unveil unseen, existential gaps
Between us I should be bridging. No, no.
That kind of intimacy I should wait
On a sign from you to engage to seek,
Don't you think? Insidious, how respect
Rights me back like conventional ballast,
But that's the latest. The rich get richer,
The busy ever more efficient. Cranks
Get up to more tricks they ought to unlearn.

South San Francisco

We're short once more folks who've learned how to track,
As wild game quit the known demographies
For whatever ancient cover remains.
Who you are and how you mean to prove it,
Twin initiatives with independent
Endowments, were supposed to parallel
One another within shouting distance,
However hand and thought and speech diverge.

Of the above, none stages tragedy,
Not even faces of the tired poor
Always, although some great replication,
Bisecting each line, and each half again,
Doubling like a chain of Spanish missions,
Configures good, and bad, and ghosts unknown.

Standard Time

Persons for whom normal rhymes are faithful
Arrive like species and varieties
In the Victorian, pre-document
Management software senses of those codes.
Meantime, scheduled numbers spill like apples
In the harvest of diligent customs,
Implicating key pad access controls
That stymie the CFO locked outside.

At closing, the volley will demand less
And we'll be free to attend the solstice
With full complement of apprehension
For orange light swimming off backyard trees.
Framed in the quiet that straddles time zones,
The still life recedes, lined with active care.

Surface Mining

You have to ask what the sovereign would think.
She's been abstracted into all of us,
Into a cacophony of silence,
Usually, but things geological
Are getting scraped from the floor, the basement,
Yea, even unto arenas beneath
Our test holes. Strata of clay compacted
Volcanically interrupted the bed
We hoped to rest our aqueous waste in,
Making plans costly, nigh unfeasible,
Taking us back through the reclamation
Process and gamuts of designations.
We will do what we can to restore, make
Ready for approved, subsequent uses.

Tender Offer

Visionaries issue a letter of
Nonbinding broad intent, to be reduced
Later to decimaled propositions,
Troubling our behavior, letting us feel
Up-sized to the point of role confusion.
Our walled-in databases spring outside
Constituencies and we need to hit
Civic hangouts to seem local again.

All of this repacks your motivation
Like hardware resqueezed into styrofoam,
Leaving you cold with the plug in your hand.
So staged, with all the thrill of unplanning
Which way the gate will swing, next week finds you
Lighting critical paths, noncompeting.

A Troubled Country Heard From

Freak error in the charter document
Spells out a sparring of doctrinaire right
Against common sense. The way the mother
Country would have handled such appalling
Discontent would have been to recycle
The whole parchment, the more fungible thing
There being thought rather than citizen.
But our people need something to believe.
Even to the point denominations
Schism at civil, nonsectarian
War is how dangerous the politics
Here can be. Often, waiting Roosevelts
In the wings have mustered what, when, needed,
Powder wigging profiles fit to be coined.

Up Against It

And when it came time to reach for the stars
Or pass out free parks department lunches,
Fathers were there, in that "now I feel it"
Emotional state that today's women
Wince at, accept or ignore, depending
On the individual in question,
Her willingness to suspend disbelief
From the closely-kept, permanent roster.

Not that I doubt my own movement to tears,
Or my fear that my fears may win the hand
In faith I'm either holding or dealing.
Imagine one moment that deepest space
Is welled within us, farthest distances
The hurts we propel, that might have been friends.

Very Nearly Yours

The answer worked the question, avoided
Omission but emphasized the bright side,
Lining an outskirt pocket with jealous
Silver, often, as is sometimes the risk
With these underwritings, however firm
The bare shelves bear against their emptiness,
That lack of a load against which to brace
That nth force physicists just discovered
But acrobats have tossed around for years.
The run is on, and the stores are sanguine
As it happens. Shelvers unzip cartons
To remark the depletion. It is meant
That the cycle be a programmatic
Replenishment of good, our stock in trade.

What You're Willing to Do

Frankly, little consequential happened,
Nothing that couldn't be fixed tomorrow,
As though the day had better purposes
Than what might be designed in increments.

Thoughts were accurate to a hard measure.
Seven directions equaled four, or four
Seven; the currency was revalued
In the cold, paperless spin of it all.

Just yesterday discovered absorption
More like adherence on a sand-fine scale.
Lunacy bubbled out of the jet set,
And crucial tasks could be turned out like probes.

Scouring the great land of this postulate,
Today we might flip the run of the road.